DO NOT REMOVE
CARDS FROM POCKET

ALLEN COUNTY PUBLIC LIBRARY

FORT WAYNE, INDIANA 46802

You may return this book to any agency, branch,
or bookmobile of the Allen County Public Library.

DEMCO

Books by Mildred Tengbom

Is Your God Big Enough?
The Bonus Years
Table Prayers
Fill My Cup, Lord
No Greater Love: The Story of Clara Maass
A Life to Cherish
Especially for Mother
Sometimes I Hurt
Does Anyone Care How I Feel?
Why Don't I Feel Good All the Time?
Devotions for New Mothers
Help for Bereaved Parents
Help for Families of the Terminally Ill
*Why Waste Your Illness? Let God Use It for
    Growth*
Bible Reading for Families

MEALTIME Prayers

*New Prayers,
Old Favorites,
Songs, &
Responses*

Mildred Tengbom

AUGSBURG Publishing House • Minneapolis

MEALTIME PRAYERS

Copyright © 1985 Augsburg Publishing House

Library of Congress Cataloging in Publication Data

Tengbom, Mildred.
  MEALTIME PRAYERS.

  1. Grace at meals—Christianity.   2. Prayers.
3. Children—Prayer-books and devotions—English.
I. Title.
BV283.G7T39   1985   242'.8   85-9041
ISBN 0-8066-2127-3

Manufactured in the U.S.A.   APH 10-4306

1   2   3   4   5   6   7   8   9   0   1   2   3   4   5   6   7   8   9

7080033

Contents

Acknowledgments

Appreciation is expressed to publishers and individuals for their permission to use material cited below. Every effort has been made to locate the source and secure permission for use of material included in this volume. Inadvertent omissions should be called to the attention of the publisher.

The prayer "God cares for me in many ways" by Eleanor Zimmerman is from *Children in God's World*, published by the Board of Publication, Lutheran Church in America. Used by permission.

The prayers by Esther Mulbah, Sabine Ruckmann, Nelson and Anna Dumeni, Elsa Gonzalez Lasalle, a Liberian youth, Fabia Suga, and Neusa Suzana Wahlbrinch are from *Children in Conversation with God*, edited by Anza A. Lema, copyright © 1979 Lutheran World Federation. Used by permission.

The prayer "Lord of tree and forest fire" by Herbert F. Brokering is from *Lord, I Want to Celebrate*, © 1980 Concordia Publishing House. Used by permission.

The prayers "We are awake," "Creator Lord, through whom everything on this earth grows," "We thank you, Lord. That was such a good meal," and "O Lord, the meal is steaming before us" by young Ghanian Christians are from *I Lie on My Mat and Pray: Prayers by Young Africans*, Fritz Pawelzik, editor, Friendship Press, N.Y., copyright 1964. Used by permission.

The prayer "Lord, bless our meal as we partake" from Italy is from *Children's Prayers around the World,* edited by Helen Clarke, © 1959 by Christian Children's Fund. Used by permission.

The prayers "O Lord, may this home be blessed" from Algeria and ". . . This day, this night, these fruits, these flowers" from Pakistan are from *Book of Children's Prayers,* compiled by William I. Kaufman, published by UNICEF, used by permission of William I. Kaufman.

The prayer "God gives summer and rain" by Marie Pooler is from *A Child Sings,* copyright © 1958 Augsburg Publishing House.

The prayer "O loving Lord, who on a still dark night" by Arthur Rouner Jr. is from the book *Someone's Praying, Lord* by Arthur A. Rouner Jr., © 1970 by Arthur A. Rouner Jr., published by Prentice-Hall, Inc., Englewood Cliffs, N.J. 07632. Used by permission.

The tune for "God Is Great, God Is Good" by Marie Pooler is copyright © Augsburg Publishing House.

The prayers "Open the shutters and trim your pale light," "Dear God, on the arms of prayer," and "We dare not carry it alone" by Gertrude Hanson are used by permission of Miles P. Evans.

The prayer "I've pinned up the calendar, Lord" by Catherine Brandt is from *Still Time to Sing,* copyright © 1980 Augsburg Publishing House.

The prayer "O Christ, deep were your wounds and red" by William Johnson is used by permission of William Johnson.

Acknowledgments

The songs "Alleluia, Thank You, O Lord" and "Thank Him" by Sheryl Monroe and Becky Mortvedt are used by permission of Sheryl Monroe and Becky Mortvedt.

The song "Thank the Lord and Sing His Praise" is copyright © 1978 *Lutheran Book of Worship.*

The prayer "Blessed art thou, O Lord" by James Qualben is used by permission of James Qualben.

The texts for "We Thank Thee, Dear Father, for Thy Gifts of Love," "Thou Gracious Giver," and "Be Present Here" by Mary Youngman Wilson are used by permission of Mary Youngman Wilson.

The text for "Heavenly Father, Kind and Good" by Eoline Kowierschke is used by permission of Eoline Kowierschke.

PRAYERS
FOR
SMALL
CHILDREN

*B*efore we eat this food, dear Lord,
we bow our heads to pray;
and for your blessings and your care
our humble thanks we say. Amen.

●

*T*hank you, heavenly Father,
for my bread,
my dad and mother and my bed. Amen.

●

*T*each me, Father, when I pray
not to ask for more,
but rather let me give my thanks
for what is at my door.
For food and drink
and gentle rain,
for sunny skies above,
for home and friends,
for peace and joy,
but most of all, for love. Amen.

*G*reat God, we praise your gracious care,
You do our daily bread prepare;
O bless the earthly food we take
and feed our souls, for Jesus' sake. Amen.
John Cennick, 1741

•

*W*e thank you, Lord, for this our food,
for life and health, and every good;
let manna to our souls be given,
the Bread of life, sent down from heaven.
John Cennick, 1741

•

*O*ur table now with food is spread;
O God, who gives us daily bread.
Bless these your gifts unto us so
that strength of body they bestow. Amen.
Thomas Kingo, 1689

*G*ive us the food we need, dear God
to help us grow and make us strong.
Give us warm clothes for winter days,
and a home we can call our own.
Give us friends and a place to play,
kind teachers and a friendly church,
doctors to care for us when we are ill,
and a family to which we'll always belong.
These things we need, heavenly Father,
to become strong and kind and good. Amen.

●

*H*ow strong and sure my Father's care,
that 'round about me, like the air,
is with me always, ev'rywhere.
He cares for me, he cares for me.
Thank you, God. Amen.

*F*ather of ours in heav'n above,
we children thank you for your love.
Our food, our homes and all we wear,
tell of your daily, loving care. Amen.

●

*G*od cares for me in many ways.
This is how I know:
the food I eat,
the clothes I wear,
friendly helpers everywhere,
say, "You are in God's care."

I must give my thanks to God
for all the love he shows:
for food to eat,
clothes to wear,
for friendly helpers everywhere,
dear God, I give my thanks. Amen.
Eleanor Zimmerman

We thank you, God:
for bakers and butchers,
for farmers and truck drivers,
for box boys and cashiers,
for supermarket managers
and those who harvest crops,
for all the many people who work
to bring food to our table,
we thank you, God. Amen.

●

Gracious Giver of all good,
we thank you for rest and food;
grant that all we do or say
may serve you joyfully today.
Amen.

*T*o you, O Lord, our hearts we raise,
for blessings filling all our days.
Each morn our wants are satisfied
with food your love and care provide.
Amen.

●

O give us hearts to thank you
for every blessing sent.
And whatsoe'er you send to us
make us therewith content. Amen.

What God gives, and what we take,
　'tis a gift for Christ, his sake;
be the meal of beans and peas,
God be thanked for those and these;
have we meat or have we fish,
all are fragments from his dish.
God be praised and thanked!

PRAYERS
BY
CHILDREN

*L*ord God, our Father in heaven, I pray to you this day to forgive my sins. I am a child, but I also know that I am a sinner. Sometimes I do things which my mother tells me I should not do. I pray for my mother and my father too. I want my father to love my mother so that we can all stay together. I pray for my country and our leaders. Help them to be just and not to cheat the poor. I pray for our teachers that they may be patient with us and teach us the right things. Give us peace in the world. Amen.

> *Prayer of Esther Mulbah, Liberia, West Africa*

G od, thank you for helping so that I can be in a good school. My school even has religion classes which is what I most wanted. Please make it possible for me always to have good schools like this. May my mother be able to pay for water, food, house and school. Make me always happy and forgive my sins. Amen.

Prayer of Sabine Ruckmann,
9 years old, Brazil

●

J esus, pacify the war in our country.
Jesus, our friend, we ask you
to protect all who are sick,
and those in prison.
We pray for all the children
who do not attend Sunday School.
We pray also for all the children
who do not know how to pray.
Dear Jesus, be with all these children
and bless and keep us all. Amen.

Prayer of Nelson and Anna Dumeni,
10 year-old twins, Namibia

I thank you for having freed us from world wars and I ask that you would bring peace to the world because it is so painful to know that there are children in the world who are losing their parents. Illuminate the minds and understanding of those who are to blame for the wars so that they know what they are doing. I ask you because I know you can do everything. Amen.

> *Prayer of Elsa Gonzlez Lasalle,*
> *Puerto Rico*

•

*D*ear Lord, I try to study hard but when tests are given, I don't make good grades. Why? I know my teacher is sometimes cruel. He takes points out for every little mistake. Sometimes I think he does that for my own good, but sometimes I am not so sure. I pray you to help me understand my problem so that I can pass. I don't want my Pa and Ma to be angry with me every time I fail. So help me to study and know. Amen.

> *Prayer of a Liberian youth.*

*L*ord, this morning I had fresh bread, coffee, juice and an egg, and every morning it continues like this. Lord, thank you for this. By the way, I want to thank you for everything, for the food that you give me, for my school, for my kind family and for my friends and clothes. Lord, I know that you like me because you gave me life. Let all of us be very happy. And help me never more to want to fight with those whom I like or don't like. So be it, for I know you want that everybody would follow your laws. Amen.

> *Prayer of Fabia Suga,*
> *Sao Paulo, Brazil*

*D*ear Father in heaven, I thank you for being such a kind parent. I thank you for all the blessings you have poured upon me and for all the happiness I have every day. I also thank you for having parents that love me and that I can also love them. I thank you for brothers and sisters with whom I can play. It's a privilege many children don't have. Finally I want to thank you for the difficulties and sufferings in my life, as they help me to become more mature and loving. Amen.

> *Prayer of Neusa Suzana Wahlbrinch*
> *12 years old, Brazil*

SENTENCE PRAYERS

For food, life, clothing, opportunities, friendships and fellowship we thank you, O Lord. Amen.

•

O God, our Creator, you give us food for the body and truth for the mind. Nourish and enlighten us so we may grow strong and become wise to do your will. Amen.

•

Benevolent and loving heavenly Father, you fill the hungry with good things and satisfy the desire of every living thing. We return our thanks through Jesus Christ our Lord. Amen.

•

Oh, Lord, root out any spirit of complaining and transplant instead the seeds of gratitude and thanksgiving in our hearts. Amen.

Oh God, grant that we who are your
children and eat of your bread may gladly
bear one another's burdens with sincere
love. Amen.

●

For all the blessings of our daily life we give
you thanks, O God. With this food
strengthen us to do your will through Christ.
Amen.

For friends to cherish, work to do, hills to climb, coats to warm us and food to nourish us, we humbly and gratefully thank you. Amen.

●

Our loving God, as we meet around this table our hearts unite in praising you for daily blessings. Amen.

●

For life preserved and strength renewed, we praise and magnify your name, O holy Lord. Amen.

We are happy to gather around this table, Lord, not only because of the food which will satisfy our hunger, but also because we can sit with those we love. We thank you, Father. Amen.

●

Gracious, loving God, bless this food to our use and us to your service, through Christ Jesus our Lord. Amen.

●

O Christ, may the strength that comes through the food you give us enable us to do your will. Amen.

Blessed are you, O Lord, our God, King of the universe, who brings forth food from the earth. Hallelujah! Amen.

●

Bless us, O Lord, and these gifts which we are about to receive from your hand. Amen.

PRAYERS
OF
PRAISE AND
THANKSGIVING

*A*lmighty and holy God,
we thank you for
your goodness, never-ending,
your will, sometimes so baffling,
your love, constant and unchanging,
your mercy, always compassionate,
your forgiveness, offered freely,
and your nurture of us,
tender and solicitous.

Our heavenly Father, we thank you that you
never leave off creating and providing for us.
Even as it is the nature of fire always to
burn, and snow always to chill, so it is part
of your nature to continue to love and
provide for us. We worship and adore you.
Amen.

*F*or everything that brings pleasure
and comfort to us,
we thank you, O loving God.
For soap that cleanses us,
work that provides for us,
food that satisfies us,
water that refreshes us,
heat that warms us,
families that care about us,
the Savior who forgives us,
the Lord who leads us,
and the Holy Spirit who empowers us.
Benevolent and loving heavenly Father,
for all these good things,
we thank you. Amen.

●

*I*mmutable God, in this world of rapid
change, we lift our hearts in praise and
thanksgiving for those things in life which
remain constant, and most of all for the
assurance of your ever-present, unchanging
love and care for us. Amen.

*L*ord of all nations, once more we lift our voices in praise and thanksgiving for all the renewed mercies which we experience as your gracious and undeserved gift to us. Humbly we thank you that you placed us in that portion of all earth where to such an extraordinary degree we may enjoy personal comfort, liberty of person, security of property, and are able to pass day after day in abundance and peace. May our hearts be filled with continual gratitude to you, our benevolent and unwearied Benefactor. May we also remember the obligations which rest upon us, because we have received so much. Amen.

*G*reat God, who made a world that gives to us the best of everything and who has placed within our hearts a longing for you, we lift our hearts in praise and worship. We thank you for all your love and mercy and pray that the hour around our table will deepen our appreciation for all you do for us. Amen.

●

*B*lessed Lord, we around this table thank you for your love, not dependent upon any worthiness of ours, for a land able to supply bountifully all our needs, for family and friends to love and care for us, and for the joy of sharing what we have with others. Amen.

*C*reator Spirit, we lift our hearts in praise
and thanksgiving for playful children
who brighten our lives with laughter,
understanding people who love us when we
are unlovable, appreciative employers who
value our work and pay us for it, wise older
people who give us perspective on our
problems.

We thank you also for hope that sustains us
in spite of a doubtful future, dreams and
plans that ever beckon us on even when
momentarily we are frustrated.

Most of all we praise and thank you for
Jesus, our Savior, who lived and died and
lives again to bring life to us.

For all these gifts and more we lift our
hearts in gratitude and praise. Amen.

MORNING
PRAYERS

*L*oving God, we gather this morning and ask your blessing on our home and your guidance for each one during the hours of this day. Help us to realize your nearness to us. Help us to be kind to those with whom we talk, industrious in our work, and unselfish in sharing ourselves and our time. Thank you that we can be assured that you will be with each of us through all the hours of this day. With gratitude we receive now our food and thank you for it. Amen.

A morn pristine and pure greets us,
we praise you, O our Lord.
With courage, strength and hope renewed
we sound the joyful chord.

On good and evil, Lord, your sun
is rising now on all.
Let us in patience and in love
seek to obey your call.

May we in virtue and in faith
and with your gifts content,
rejoice beneath your covering wings,
each day in mercy sent.

Safe with your counsel in your word,
you, Lord, we'll keep in view.
And know that still your saving grace
is every morning new.

Johan Olaf Wallin, 1816, (altered)

*G*od, our Provider, we know it is both
your love and grace and the willingness
of people to work that brings food to our
table. Help us, this day, to do our daily
work patiently and faithfully, especially
when work seems routine and unimportant.
If big responsibilities come our way, give us
courage and faith to accept them. And if
illness or unemployment keep us from
gainful work, help us through those difficult
times too, even as we pray for restored
health and reimbursed work. In Christ's
name, we pray. Amen.

•

*A*s we begin another day
give us, O Lord of all hopefulness,
awareness of your presence,
insight into our problems,
humility to acknowledge our need,
willingness to seek your help,
trust to believe you will act
on our behalf,
and gratitude for all you are
and do for us. Amen.

O Lord and maker of all things, when the world's first morning dawned, you looked upon it and said it was good. Now as the light of a new day creeps into our home help us to face this day with praise and declare, It is good to be alive!

O Lord, we offer praise for the life which pulsates through our bodies, for the beauty of this world, though often we are too distracted or too busy to notice it, for the earth, our home, canopied by the sky, encircled by the oceans, spinning in space, a priceless jewel among the planets.

We thank you for clear days, for days of sunshine, days of rain and even for days of smog, for we are still alive.

We praise you also for the work you have given us to do and for the many and varied interests to pursue in leisure time.

O Light that never fades, we open to you this morning the windows of our hearts, and pray that our lives may be filled by the radiance of your presence.

May the Spirit of him whose life, like a
light, illuminated the way for all peoples
rule in our hearts until evening falls. Amen.

●

*D*ear God, take this day's events into
your keeping. Help me to discipline
all my thoughts and feelings. Enfuse me
with energy. May my mind be keen and
alert, my imagination lively, my creative
abilities sharp. Sustain my will to desire only
your will. Take my hands and make them
skillful to serve. Take my feet and may they
move quickly to obey you. Take my eyes
and help me see people and circumstances
as you see them. Take my mouth and make
it bold to protest injustice and wrong, and
tender in offering comfort and
encouragement. May this day be a day of
obedience to you, a day of peace, joy and
love. May this day, as I live it, bring glory
and honor to my Lord Jesus Christ, in
whose name I pray. Amen.

EVENING
PRAYERS

*O*ur Redeemer God, at the close of a
hectic day we turn to you for the peace
only you can give. Quieten our hearts.
(Sit quietly for a moment.)

We feel the irritations and frustrations of the
day slipping away. Thank you, God.

If we've had resentful feelings towards some
who have been difficult to live with today,
forgive us. Help us to forgive.

Set us free from a desire to get ahead of
others that will make us insensitive, cruel or
uncaring. Make us willing to think of helping
others succeed. Help us to work in
partnership, caring for each other. Forgive
us if we've complained today. Help us
instead to focus on all the blessings that are
ours and to look for rainbows. And thank
you that once again you have provided so
generously for all our needs. In Christ's
name. Amen.

O Jesus, giver of peace, if we have come to this table in turmoil, we pray that in the moments of silence now as we remind ourselves of your presence, that you will fill us with the Holy Spirit's gift of peace. (Pause for a moment of silence.) Receive from us our humble thanks for these gifts you have given to us. In your matchless name, we pray. Amen.

*L*ord Jesus, we thank you that you invite all who are weary and heavy burdened to come to you. We are tired tonight. The day made many demands on us. You know our anxieties, fears, concerns and regrets. You know about tense muscles, tired heads, aching bodies and spent minds, and you care. We thank you for food and drink which rejuvenate us. We thank you for the warm acceptance of the family circle which encourages and sustains us. We thank you for your grace and love which forgives, cleanses and restores us. For all these good gifts, accept our thanks, Lord Jesus. Amen.

PRAYERS
ON
TRUST

O Lord God, Creator of the universe, what good would the tractor be, if there was not life in the soil? What would the toil of people avail, if seeds did not have the power to sprout and produce? What meaning would a season of labor carry, if, in the end, pests, disease or storms strip the crop? We acknowledge our dependence on you. Forgive us when we have been proud and have thought smugly that we could provide for ourselves. Teach us always to look to you from whom all good things come. In Christ's name. Amen.

*I*nspire us, O God, to lift up our hearts to you, and may the Holy Spirit help us to worship in spirit and truth. We come before you, we who are continually dependent on your goodness. You brought us into existence. You supported us during our helpless years of infancy. You watched over us during our childhood, and you bore with us during our stormy years of youth. You have carried us through the various periods of our lives and have brought us through days of difficulty, trouble and sorrow. We look to you as the Author and Giver of all. We acknowledge your goodness and long suffering shown as you have borne patiently with us when we have provoked you. We desire that your love will be shed abroad in our hearts that they may be warmed with more fervent and continual gratitude to you. Amen.

*O*ur Creator God, we are completely dependent on you. No matter how great our resources, skill and knowledge, it is only because of your mercy and faithfulness in causing seeds to sprout, sun to shine, rain to fall, disaster and pests to be kept at abeyance, that we have food to eat. Help us who buy our food in supermarkets to remember this so we may accept your provision for us gratefully, but also humbly. Amen.

PRAYERS
OF
CONCERN

*O*ur Savior God,
    our heritage has been a rich one.
Our daily bread has never failed.
Remember in mercy those who hunger
and may we never forget
that your kingdom on earth
must come through us, your children.
Amen.

●

*G*od of rock and fern, God of rain and
    sunshine, God of the butterfly and the
bear, God of asphalt cities and mountain
slopes, we accept with gratitude all the gifts
the earth you created gives us. Give us
wisdom to work in partnership with you in
caring for the earth. Help us to be good
stewards of our spaceship earth, our first but
present home. Amen.

*A*lmighty God, everlasting Father, we stand in awe at the mystery of life. We thank you that you cause the seeds to sprout, the rain to fall, the sun to shine, and the crops to grow. We are dependent on your love and fidelity. We thank you. We pray also that you would have mercy on those who live in areas where the forces of nature have turned against them, where they experience drought or floods or pests that destroy. As you have blessed and provided bountifully for us, so give us hearts that will find joy in sharing what you have freely given us. In Christ's name, we pray. Amen.

O God of mercy, we cannot understand
why we are the favored ones,
why all of our needs are provided
while others are oppressed with need.
We could have been born in another land.
We pray for all
who lack food and clothing,
who are cold and ill,
who have lost home and country,
who are disheartened and discouraged,
who are unemployed or underemployed.
Give us the will and provide the grace
to love them all in you
and in loving to help bear their burdens
and meet their needs.
In Christ's name, we pray. Amen.

*C*reator God, you give and give to us.
You give even when you don't receive
anything from us in return. We stand in awe
of your love that never gets tired of giving.
The food we have before us is just one small
token of how you love to give. Teach us, O
Father, not to hoard love, money, time or
possessions. Teach us to give without
thought of receiving (how hard this is!).
Teach us to give, not just things, but
ourselves, to those we love and to others
who need our love. May what we give
become our visible thank you to you for all
you give to us. Amen.

*L*ord, forgive us when we are concerned with insignificant things and neglect that which is of concern to you.
Forgive us for tolerating unfair distribution of the gifts of the earth you have given us.
Forgive us for allowing laws that prevent people from living in dignity and liberty.
Forgive us for low ideals, for racial prejudice and for disregard of the needs of the poor.
Forgive us for broken homes, neglected children and abandoned old people.
Help us to realize our complete dependence on you and always to receive your provision with humility and thankfulness. Amen.

PRAYERS
FOR A
CLOSER WALK
WITH GOD

*G*od of mercies, in your word you have said that we should consider it pure joy whenever we face trials of many kinds. We confess that we have found this difficult to do. We come to you asking that you would cleanse us from all that sours us and makes us react negatively to people and life. We pause before you now. We want to accept from you with thanks all that is making us miserable. *(Observe a moment of silent prayer.)* Benevolent Giver, we ask you now to give us the strength, courage and ability to meet the special needs we bring before you now. *(Observe a moment of silent prayer.)* Gracious God, we want to drink richly of life and savor carefully all its blessings. We pause before you now. We remember with thanksgiving all your mercies toward us. *(Observe a moment of silent prayer.)* Have your way in our lives. We pray in our Savior's name. Amen.

O God, most judicious giver of all gifts,
we thank you for the unexpected
surprises with which you astonish us. How
discreetly you give! Set us free to enjoy
every cup of sweetness you offer us. And if
the contents of our cup should turn to
bitterness, enable us to rest content in your
love, trusting you even for that which we
cannot understand now. In your Son's name,
who suffered and gave his all for us, we
pray, Amen.

*G*od, my Creator and Redeemer,
I confess

my insensitivity and indifference to the suffering of others and my unwillingness to be taught by my own suffering;

my complacence toward injustices I feel not directed towards me and my resentment when I have been mistreated;

my reluctance to see the good in my fellow-pilgrims, and my tendency to defend myself when others point out wrong in me;

my judgmental attitude towards my neighbor's faults, and my readiness to make excuses for my own;

my petulant pouting and destructive jealousy when I hear of others succeeding and my own small successes seem overshadowed by frequent failures;

my unwillingness to accept that you have called others to positions of greater honor, praise and prominence and given to me an obscure task of little-recognized or seldom-appreciated service;

O Lord, for all this, forgive me and cleanse me. Amen.

*A*lmighty Creator God, you hold the whole world in your hand. The five continents, the sun and moon and all the vast universe, the rivers, oceans and seas, the cities and prairies, all are yours, O God.

And this world you have entrusted to our stewardship. Give us wisdom to care for it. Implant within our hearts awe and gratitude for the stupendous trust you have placed in us. Forgive us when we take our world for granted.

Take our voices to awaken concern for your world and to sing your praises. Take our hearts to love those who are in need. Take our hands to work, to serve, and to care tenderly, both for others and your world.

Only as we do this, can we with a glad and free heart receive the food you have given us. In Christ's name. Amen.

*B*rightness of the Father's glory
and image of his being,
renew in us your holy likeness.
Light of the world,
illumine our way.
Eternal life,
give us life in you.
Prince of Peace,
bring peace to our hearts
and to the world.
Bread of life,
feed us with bread for body and soul.
Amen.

●

*O*ur Father, you know how disappointed
we feel when we give gifts to someone,
and the gifts are not received with
appreciation. But how often, Father, we
receive your gifts with little visible joy or
delight. Forgive us. May your gifts to us
never become commonplace. Restore in us a
child's sense of wonder and make us always
truly grateful. Amen.

O Jesus, you have called us
to be your disciples:
to follow you,
live for you,
witness for you,
suffer for you,
work for you,
get tired for you,
wear out for you,
and probably even die for you.
To this end we dedicate ourselves
as we receive the food we need
in order to live. Amen.

•

Great and glorious God, we lift up our
hearts to you. We owe all we have and
all we are to you, O Lord. You have bound
us to yourself by ten thousand obligations.
Oh, that we might love you more, and be
more grateful! We ask your mercy and grace
in the name of and for the sake of Jesus
Christ, our Savior. Amen.

O God, our loving Provider,
you give food for the body
truth for the mind
and forgiveness for the spirit.
Teach and instruct us
that we may grow wise and strong
and live lives that will please you.
In Christ's name, Amen.

PRAYERS
FROM
LONG AGO

O Lord Jesus Christ, Good Shepherd of the sheep, who came to seek the lost and to gather them into your fold, have compassion on those who have wandered from you; feed those who hunger, cause the weary to lie down in your pastures, bind up those who are broken in heart, and strengthen those who are weak, that we, relying on your care and being comforted by your love, may abide in your guidance to our lives' end.

> *Ancient Collect*
> *Sixth Century*

•

A lmighty and everlasting God, be present with us in all our duties and grant the protection of your presence to all who dwell in this house, that you may be known to be the Defender of this household and the Inhabitant of this dwelling.

> *Gelasian Sacramentary*
> *Sixth Century*

*L*ord, when we look upon our own lives,
it seems Thou hast led us so carefully,
so tenderly, Thou canst have attended to no
one else. But when we see how wonderfully
Thou hast led the world and art leading it,
we are amazed that Thou hast time to attend
to such as we. We praise and thank Thee.

    Augustine

●

*T*hou, O Lord, provideth enough for all
men with Thy most liberal and
bounteous hand, but whereas Thy gifts are,
in respect to Thy goodness and free favor,
made common to all men, we, through our
naughtiness, selfishness and distrust, do
make them private and peculiar. Correct
thou the thing which our iniquity hath put
out of order, and let Thy goodness supply
that which our selfishness hath plucked
away.

    Queen Elizabeth I's Prayer Book,
    Sixteenth Century

O God, our Father, we thank you for all the bright things of life. Help us to see them and to count them and to remember them that our lives may flow in ceaseless praise. For the sake of Jesus Christ our Lord, Amen.

> *J. H. Jowett*

●

O Lord, our God, teach us to ask for the right blessings. Steer the vessel of our life towards yourself, you who are the tranquil haven of all storm-tossed souls. Show us the course wherein we should go. Renew a willing spirit within us. Let your spirit curb our wayward desires and guide and enable us toward that which is our true good. In all our work enable us to rejoice in your glorious and gladdening presence. For yours is the glory and the praise forever and ever. Amen.

> *St. Basil*

O heavenly Father, you have filled the world with beauty and provided for us in abundance. Open our eyes to behold your gracious hand in all your works; that rejoicing in your whole creation, we may learn to serve you with gladness.

> Book of Common Prayer
> *Sixteenth Century*

●

O Christ be with us. Be before us, after us and in us. O Christ, be on our right hand, on our left hand, on this side, on that side and at our back. May everyone to whom we speak and every person who speaks to us today, hear you, O Christ. May every person who looks upon us, see you, O Christ. May every person who hears us today, hear you, O Christ. May you be glorified in us. Amen.

> *St. Patrick (altered)*

*B*less all who are members of this family,
from the rising of the sun
unto the going down of the same.
Of your goodness, give us;
with your love, inspire us;
by your spirit, guide us;
with your power, protect us;
in your mercy, receive us
now and always. Amen.

Ancient Collect

●

*A*lmighty God, our heavenly Father,
whose mercies are new unto us every
morning, and who, though we have in no
way deserved your goodness, do abundantly
provide for all our wants of body and soul:
fill us, we pray, with the Holy Spirit, that
we may heartily acknowledge your merciful
goodness toward us, give thanks for all your
benefits, and serve you in willing obedience;
through Jesus Christ, your Son, our Lord.
Amen.

*L*ord, we do not know what we ought to ask of you; you only know best what we need. You love us better than we know how to love ourselves. O Father, give to us, your children, that which we ourselves do not know to ask. We have no other desire than to accomplish your will. Teach us to pray, and pray through us; for Christ's sake. Amen.

Francois Fenelon

P leasure it is
to hear
the birdes sing,
the deer in the dale,
the sheep in the vale,
the corn springing.
God's provision
for sustenance
it is for all.
Then we always
to him give praise,
and thank him then,
and thank him then.

William Cornish, England,
Sixteenth Century

*T*hrough every month your gifts appear,
   Great God, your goodness crowns the
year!
   Isaac Watts

●

*B*less, O Lord, this house and all who
   dwell in it, as you were pleased to bless
the house of Abraham, Isaac and Jacob; that
within these walls may dwell an angel of
light, and that we who dwell together in it
may receive the abundant dew of heavenly
blessing and through your tenderness rejoice
in peace and quiet.

   Gelasian Sacramentary
   Sixth Century

O Father, our whole life has been one great proof of your care. Bread has come for our bodies, thoughts to our minds, love to our hearts, and all from you. May this day be full of a power that shall bring us near to you, and make us more like you; and, O God, may we so trust you this day that when the day is done our trust shall be firmer than ever.

> *Robert Collyer, Wales*
> *Nineteenth Century*

*G*racious God, Ruler of the world
and loving Savior of all,
Let there be righteousness in the heart,
so there will be beauty in the character.
Let there be beauty in the character,
so there will be harmony in the home.
Let there be harmony in the home,
so there will be order in the nation.
Let there be order in the nation,
so there will be peace in the world.

> *Adapted from an old Chinese*
> *proverb*

*H*allowed be Thy name.
In industry:
God be in my hands and in my making.
In the arts:
God be in my senses and in my creating.
In the home:
God be in my heart and in my loving.
In commerce:
God be at my desk and in my trading.
In suffering:
God be in my pain and in my enduring.
In government:
God be in my plans and in my deciding.
In education:
God be in my mind and in my growing.
In recreation:
God be in my limbs and in my leisure.
Holy, holy, holy, Lord God of hosts,
Heaven and earth are full of Thy glory.

> *From prayer panels in the ruins*
> *of Coventry Cathedral*

PRAYERS
OF
TODAY

O gracious Father, for so many years and
through so many seasons of life you
have provided for us. May our relationship
with you never become commonplace. Help
us instead always to look beyond our plates
and beyond the remembrances of your grace
and love into your face and be at peace.
Amen.

●

*M*ay I seek to live this day
quietly serenely,
leaning on your mighty strength
trustfully, restfully,
meeting others in the path
peacefully, joyously,
waiting for your will's unfolding
patiently, obediently,
facing what tomorrow brings
confidently, courageously.

Author unknown

RESPONSIVE PRAYERS

*L*ord Jesus, you gave thanks before
you ate.
  R/ *Help us always to eat with*
    gratitude.
You pronounced all food clean.
  R/ *Help us to enjoy and relish*
    all food.
You commanded the disciples to feed
the hungry multitude,
  R/ *Motivate us to help provide for*
    the hungry of today.
You saved a family from embarrassment by
providing wine for the wedding feast,
  R/ *Provide for us too so we may be*
    able to celebrate appropriately
    the festival events of life.

You became so absorbed in your
Father's work that
you paid little
attention to your hunger.
   *R/ Infuse us with the same zeal
      to do your will.*
You always bore patiently with the
fraility of your human friends.
   *R/ Help us to be patient with each
      other.*
You became known to your disciples as
you broke bread with them.
   *R/ Reveal yourself also to us as we
      break bread together now.*

*F*or all good things the Lord has given
us, let us praise him.
  R/ *For all sweet things, we praise*
     you, O Lord.
Oranges and apples,
Honey and jam,
Hot chocolate fudge sauce
and juicy red strawberries,
All/ we praise you, O Lord.
  R/ *For all soft things, we praise you,*
     O Lord.
Mashed potatoes,
Ripe bananas
Creamy chocolate pudding
and smooth avocadoes,
All/ we praise you, O Lord.
  R/ *For all crunchy things, we*
     praise you, O Lord.

Crackers and pretzels,
Peanuts and raw carrots,
Crisp cold celery
and healthful granola,
All/ we praise you, O Lord.
   *R/ For all spicey things, we
        praise you, O Lord.*
Red pepper and salsa sauce,
Curried meat and spaghetti sauce,
Lasagne, hot tamales and burritos,
All/ we praise you, O Lord.
   *R/ For all nutritious, tasty,
        delectable food which is lavishly
        provided for us day after day,*
All/ we praise you, O Lord.

We plow the fields and scatter
the good seed on the land,
but it is fed and watered
by God's almighty hand.
He sends the snow in winter
the warmth to swell the grain,
the breezes and the sunshine
and soft refreshing rain.
> R/ *All good gifts around us*
> *are sent from heaven above.*
> *Then thank the Lord,*
> *oh, thank the Lord, for all his love.*

We thank you, our Creator
for all things bright and good.
The seedtime and the harvest,
our life, our health, our food.
No gifts have we to offer
for all your love imparts,
but what you most would treasure
our humble, thankful hearts.
> R/ *All good gifts around us*
> *Are sent from heaven above.*
> *Then thank the Lord,*
> *oh, thank the Lord, for all his love.*

God only is the maker
of all things near and far.
He paints the wayside flower,
he lights the evening star.
The winds and waves obey him;
by him the birds are fed.
Much more, to us his children
he gives our daily bread.
> R/ *All good gifts around us*
> *are sent from heaven above.*
> *Then thank the Lord,*
> *oh, thank the Lord, for all his love.*

Matthias Caludius, 1740-1815
tr. Jane M. Campbell 1817-78

*G*od of all good,
we cannot live without you.
   R/ *Care for us tenderly.*
We are tired.
   R/ *Refresh us.*
We are hungry.
   R/ *Feed us.*
We are thirsty.
   R/ *Satisfy the longings of our hearts.*
We are often forgetful.
   R/ *Remind us of your never failing*
      loving-kindness.
We are weak.
   R/ *Strengthen us.*
We faint because of the "everydayness" of
life.
   R/ *Help us to appreciate the value*
      of routine and schedule.
We are sometimes careless at school or
work.
   R/ *Make us conscious that we serve*
      the Lord of heaven and earth.
Above all, we pray,
may our love for you grow and grow,
until it overflows in wonder,
worship, awe and praise.

PRAYERS
FROM
OTHER LANDS

We are awake.
     Sleep is still in our eyes,
but at once on our lips
shall be your praise.
We glorify, praise and adore you.
The earth, the water and the sky;
the grasses and bushes and trees;
the birds and all the other animals;
the people here on earth.
Everything that you have created
enjoys your sun
and your grace
and becomes warm in it.
Dawn glistens on the grasses.
Mist is still hanging in the trees,
and a soft wind
promises a fine day.
Should we not enjoy everything
that you have created?
We are meant to.
That is why we are so joyful this
     morning, O Lord.
Grant that the hours and minutes
do not slip away in our hands,
but that we live in your time. Amen.

Prayer of a young Ghanaian
Christian

*C*reator Lord,
   through whom everything
on this earth grows—
sweet bananas, fat plantains,
sour oranges, dry yams,
rice, corn and peanuts
from which this good soup is squeezed—
who let the sharp red peppers grow
that keep us healthy
and burn stomachs clean;
who let fresh water burst from the
   ground,
good, fresh water . . .
Bless for us this meal,
our loving God and Father.
Amen.

> *Prayer of a young Ghanaian*
> *Christian*

We thank you, Lord.
 That was such a good meal.
The soup was good.
The meat was good.
The hot pepper and the yam were good.
O Lord, our stomachs are full.
Our bodies have what they need.
This is a new miracle every day.
We thank you for it
and also for the good taste
that lingers on our tongues.
How refreshing your water was!
With this meal you gave us
the strength required for the day.
Add to it your Spirit
so that we might use our strength
  rightly.
Give us, besides food for our bodies,
your heavenly food
for our whole life.
Praised be you, merciful God.
Amen.

> *Prayer of a young Ghanaian
> Christian*

O Lord,
the meal is steaming before us,
and it smells good.
The water is clear and fresh.
We are happy and satisfied.
But now we must think of our sisters
    and brothers
all over the world
who have nothing to eat
and only little to drink.
Please, please give all of them your
    food
and your drink.
That is most important.
But give them also
what they need every day
to go through this life.
As you gave food and drink
to the people of Israel in the desert
please give it also
to our hungry and thirsty brothers and
    sisters
now, and in all times.
Amen.

> *Prayer of a young Ghanaian
> Christian*

O God,
I am as one hungry for rice,
parched as one thirsty for tea.
Fill my so empty heart. Amen.

> *China*

●

O Lord,
as the cherry blossoms
quickly fall and are forgotten,
so in your bounteous mercy
grant that our sins may be shed
and remembered no more.

> *Japan*

*T*emper my character, O Father.
I want to be a real Christian.
Teach me this day to be as wholly meek
and humble as the weeping willow,
and as heroically straight and strong
as the snow-enduring bamboo. Amen.

Japan

●

L ord, bless our meal
As we partake
Of fruits of land and sea.
And let them make us strong and well
The better to serve Thee.

Italy

O Lord,
may this home be blessed.
May your Word be revered here
and your commandments respected.
May all who abide here remain faithful
to your Word and to prayer.
In all of life,
only you are to be feared.
Bless us, Lord,
bless the parents of this home,
the children,
our teachers and pastors
and all our fellowmen
throughout the world.
O, our God, forgive our wrongdoings
and bring peace to our soul,
and joy and good health
to our parents who protect
and care for us.

Algeria

*G*reat Spirit, whose tepee is the sky and whose hunting ground is the earth. All-afraid-of-you-and-mighty are you called; Ruler over storms, over people and birds and beasts and mountains, Have your way over all, over earthways and skyways. Find us this day our meat and corn that we may be strong and brave; And put aside from us our wicked ways, as we put aside the bad of all who do us wrong. And let us not have troubles that lead into crooked paths; But keep everyone in our camp from all danger. For yours is all that is: the earth and sky, the streams, the hills, and the valleys, the stars, the moon, and the sun; all that live and breathe. Wonderful, shining mighty Spirit, we worship you! Amen.

*The Lord's Prayer
in North American Indian
paraphrase*

*G*od,
we thank you for all your gifts.
This day, this night,
These fruits, these flowers,
these trees, these waters—
With all these treasures
you have endowed us.
The heat of the sun,
the light of the moon,
The songs of the birds
and the coolness of the breeze,
The green, green grass
like a mattress of velvet.
All owe their existence to your grace.
Dear God, may we forever breathe
the breath of your love
And every moment be aware
of your presence above.

> *Pakistan*

PRAYERS
FOR
SPECIAL
OCCASIONS

Thanksgiving

For your gifts so many
this Thanksgiving day,
hear us, loving Father,
as we gladly say,
we thank you,
we thank you!

Louise M. Oglevee

●

Thanksgiving

God gives summer sun and rain,
fields and trees and fruit and grain.
Thank you, God, for love and care,
and for beauty ev'rywhere.

Marie Pooler

Thanksgiving

Lord of tree and forest fire,
lightning rod and 'lectric wire,
bubbling spring and ocean wave,
come and see and come to save.
Lord of snow and winter wheat,
give us milk and bread to eat.
Lord of silver, gold, and dust,
teach us how to thank and trust.

Herbert F. Brokering

●

Christmas

O loving Lord, who on a still dark night lit
only by the stars, gave in silence before
shepherds' eyes and mighty kings a tiny
Saviour to the world; we who've found our
darkness turned to light by him, our lostness
turned to life by him, and our loneliness
turned to laughter by him, give thanks and
praise for sending Jesus!

Arthur A. Rouner Jr.

Christmas

What gift shall we bring to you, O Jesus,
  this day?
You were willing to empty yourself
  and be born as a baby.
The angels bring their song.
The heavens bring their star.
The Magi bring their gifts
The shepherds bring their worship.
Bethlehem gives a cow-barn.
Joseph gives a father's care.
Mary gives her willingness to suffer
  that she may give birth to you.
And we, we, O Jesus, would give you
  the love and worship of our hearts.
O Jesus, God before all world,
  have mercy on us and receive us.
Amen.

Christmas

Today Christ is born.
Today salvation has appeared.
Today our Lord and Savior,
who has existed before all ages,
has revealed himself to the world.
We offer you praise and say,
Glory to God in the highest.
Alleluia!

Christmas

Open the shutters
  and trim your pale light;
The little Lord Jesus
  seeks shelter tonight.
Listen . . . his voice!
Have you heard it before?
The kind, loving Savior
  is nearing your door.
Quicken your steps.
  The forgiver of sin
Is there at your threshold . . .
  and wants to come in.

Gertrude Hanson

●

Christmas

Oh, come to our hearts, Lord Jesus,
There is room in our hearts for you! Amen.

New Year

I've pinned up a new calendar, Lord,
turned my back on the old year.
A year marked by failures,
times I trusted my own strength.

Lord, give me grace
this new year
to trust you.
Give me courage
to hold a garage sale
of thoughts I don't need.
Mend breaches.
Outgrow grudges,
pray with more faith.
O Christ, strengthen me.

Catharine Brandt

New Year

As we begin this new year, O God, we pray that you would draw us to yourself, incline our wills to follow you, stimulate our imaginations to creative living, enable us to keep our minds keen and pure, motivate us with compassion for the suffering and give us the common sense we need for daily living.

We dedicate ourselves anew to you and pray that your will and purpose may be fulfilled through our lives this coming year and always. In Christ's name we pray. Amen.

●

Good Friday

Lord Jesus Christ, when you stretched out your arms on the hard wood of the cross you embraced with love all people. So clothe us with your Spirit that we too, with your love, will embrace all. We ask it for your glory, Amen.

Good Friday

O Christ, deep were your wounds, and red,
on cruel Calvary,
as on the cross you bled in bitter agony.
But we, whom sin has wounded sore,
find healing in the wounds you bore.

You suffered shame and scorn,
and wretched, dire disgrace;
forsaken and forlorn, you hung there in
    our place.
But we who would from sin be free
look to your cross for victory.

Your life, your all, you gave
when you were crucified;
our burdened souls to save what fearful
    death you died!
But each of us, though dead in sin,
through you eternal life may win.

William Johnson

Easter

O Jesus, king of gentleness,
With constant love our hearts possess;
To you our lips will ever raise
The tribute of our grateful praise.
Alleluia!

O Christ, you are the Lord of all
In this our Easter festival,
For you will be our strength and shield
From ev'ry weapon death can wield.
Alleluia!

All praise, O risen Lord, we give
To you, once dead, but now alive!
To God the Father equal praise,
And God, the Holy Ghost, we raise!
Alleluia!

> *Latin hymn*
> *tr. John M. Neale*

Independence Day

Almighty God, we make our earnest prayer that you will keep the United States in thy holy protection, that you will incline the hearts of the citizens to cultivate a spirit of obedience to do what is right, and entertain affection and love for one another and for their fellow-citizens of the United States at large. And finally, that you will most graciously be pleased to incline us all to do justice, to love mercy, and to conduct ourselves with that love, humility, and peaceful temper of mind which were the characteristics of the divine Author of our blessed religion, and without a humble imitation of whose example in these things we can never hope to have a happy nation. Amen.

George Washington

Independence Day

O God, who by your providence led our forefathers to this land where they found refuge from oppression and freedom to worship you: we ask you ever to guide our nation in the way of your truth and peace, so that we may never fail in the blessing which you have promised to that people whose God is the Lord; through Jesus Christ our Lord. Amen.

Paul Zeller Strodach
Common Service of 1888.

Independence Day

We praise you, O God, for
comfortable homes,
caring people,
rapid communication,
well-stocked stores,
a stable government,
arts and music,
well-equipped hospitals,
an amazing variety of churches
schools and colleges for everyone,
and for all else that is ours
because of freedom
and your magnificent generosity,
so little deserved by us.
We thank you, even as we pray
for forgiveness and mercy
for the comfort that is ours
only because of great cost to others.
Motivate us to do justice
and live peaceably.
In Christ's name. Amen.

Labor Day

God of the nations, we pray for our nation:
may those who labor receive just and
   adequate salaries,
may employers administrate with
   consideration and integrity,
may legislators govern with honesty, wisdom
   and righteousness,
may teachers instruct through upright lives,
may lawyers interpret the law in a way
   pleasing to you,
may religious leaders guide people in the
   way of your trust, mercy, justice, and
   righteousness,
may health professionals care for the ill and
   ailing with compassion and skill,
may agriculturists tend the earth as astute
   stewards,
may those who carry on the industries and
   commerce of this land be responsive to
   your will,

may those who work in prisons and
   correctional institutions be humane and
   compassionate,
may those who create art and music reflect
   your beauty,
may judges and magistrates administer the
   law impartially as instruments of your
   divine will,
may parents have wisdom, patience and love
   as they rear their families.
Light among all of us the gentle fire of
kindliness that our nation may live in peace
and harmony. In Christ's name, Amen.

Veterans' Day

We give thanks to you, God, for all the good things our country has given to us and continues to offer us. Help us never forget that many of these blessings have been bought and paid for by human suffering and sacrifice. Save us from lightly regarding these sacrifices, but instead may we be grateful for those who in years past labored, loved, suffered, became crippled or died so we might enjoy an invaluable inheritance. We make our petition humbly and with thanksgiving. Amen.

Birthday

Dear Father, on the arms of prayer
We take _____ to you today.
For benediction of your love
Now . . . tomorrow . . . and for aye.
Open his/her eyes that he/she may read
Your guideposts set along the way,
Help him/her find refuge and content
Near . . . afar . . . and now, this day.
Steadfast and constant keep him/her,
   Lord—
Spotless and brave and true and free.
Embrace and hold him/her in your power
Now . . . today . . . eternally.
His/her body, mind and soul mold
Into a temple rich and rare;
and keep him/her for your service, Lord,
Now . . . always . . . and everywhere.

        Gertrude Hanson

Celebration on the Birth of a Child

We dare not carry it alone,
this sacred call to parenthood . . .
in humbleness we kneel to plead
For all the help that we shall need.
We pray for understanding hearts,
For courage, love, for songs to sing,
And staffs for paths that must be trod . . .
We are in partnership with God.

Gertrude Hanson

Wedding Anniversary

O God, we thank you that you so directed our lives that we found each other and together have been able to discover what it means to truly love. Let us never take each other for granted.

Continue to teach us to be courteous in speech and act, to be sensitive to know how the other one feels, to take time to know what is important to the other and then help our loved one attain treasured goals, to daily practice expressing appreciation, to share daily chores and family responsibilities, and to face all life bravely with united hearts.

Quicken within our hearts a fresh sense of romance and a spirit of praise and thanksgiving so that whatever spot on earth becomes our home, contentment, peace, harmony and joy will characterize it. In Christ's name we ask, Amen.

Graduation

O God, today we are remembering the way over which you have brought _____ to this day.

We thank you for gladness and grief, for sorrow and joy, for laughter and tears, for successes and failures, for broken hearts and rich friendships, for dreams dreamed and dreams dashed, for supportive teachers and difficult ones, for lean times and prosperous days, for silent hours and bursts of song, for all this and more, we praise and thank you, O God.

You have kept _____ in his/her going out and coming in. You have granted health

and strength to study and complete the courses. You have encouraged and kept him/her going through difficult times. We give you thanks, O God.

Give _____ wisdom for the days ahead, patience, courage and endurance.

May the beauty of the Lord our God rest upon _____ and establish and prosper the work _____ will be doing, all to your glory and honor, O God. Amen.

Mother's Day

Blessed art thou, O Lord,
Creator of the universe and our Redeemer.
Blessed are we in this house,
for you have given to us this woman
as wife and mother.
We stand and bless her
for thy name's sake.
She brings honor to this house.
She is our wealth in love
in strength and in dignity.
She does all things in lovingkindness
    and mercy.
She is our mirror of your love for us.
Blessed are we, O Lord,
for this woman.
There are many good women,
but you have chosen her for us,
and she is the best of all!
Blessed are we! Amen.

James Qualben

Mother's or Father's Day

On this day of memories,
we thank you, O God, for our parents
who listen to us,
discipline us,
spend time with us,
forgive us,
laugh and joke with us,
encourage us,
grieve when we do something wrong,
play with us,
dream with us,
show us how to work,
pray for us,
and, most of all,
love us and care about us and each other.
What a beautiful gift you have given
   us in our parents, O God.
We thank you from the bottom of our
   hearts.

When Guests Dine with Us

A circle of friends is a blessed thing.
Sweet is the breaking of bread
   with friends.
For the honor of their presence
   at our board
We are deeply grateful, Lord.

Thanks be to Thee for friendship shared,
Thanks be to Thee for food prepared.
Blessed Thou the cup; bless Thou
   the bread;
Thy blessing rest upon each head.

Walter Rauschenbusch

When Someone Leaves Home

O God, our Defender and Protector,
wherever we go we are never beyond the
circle of your care. Bless _____ as he/
she leaves home today. Send your angels to
watch over him/her. Keep him/her safe from
all harm and danger. Provide for all his/her
needs. While we are separated from each
other may no one of us do anything that
would embarrass or bring shame to our
family. Keep the fires of love we have for
each other burning brightly. And though we
are absent from each other may we always
remember that you are ever present with us.
In Christ's powerful name, we pray. Amen.

●

Family Gatherings

Bless this our family we pray.
May we cherish our bread
before there is none,
discover each other before we leave
and enjoy each other for what we are
while we have time. Amen.

When Someone Is Ill

O God, our loving heavenly Father, be with
and help _____ during this time of
illness. Give him/her courage and patience,
endurance and cheerfulness to bear
weakness, isolation and pain. Help him/her
not to worry but to trust you and the doctors
and nurses who care for him/her. Help us
not to worry but to leave our loved one in
your hands and the hands of those who are
skilled to care for the ill.

Dear God, be with our family in a special
way these days, and may we see your
healing power at work again in restoring our
loved one to health and strength. This we
ask for Christ's sake and for his glory. Amen.

PRAYERS
TO
SING

Come, Lord Jesus

Author Unknown

Hendon
Henri A. César Malan

Come, Lord Je - sus,_ be our guest. Let these gifts to_ us be_blessed. Heav'n-ly Fa-ther

bless this food_ to thy glo - ry and_our_good,_ to thy glo - ry_ and our good. A-men.

Thou Gracious Giver

Mary Youngman Wilson

Old Hundredth
Louis Bourgeois

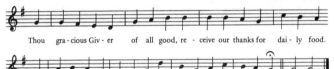

Thou gra - cious Giv - er of all good, re - ceive our thanks for dai - ly food.

Bless us and grant that we may be al - ways and ev - er close to thee. A - men.

Heavenly Father, Kind and Good

Eoline Kowierschke

Pilot
John E. Gould

Heav'n-ly Fa - ther, kind_and good, thanks we of - fer for this food. For thy

love and ten-der care, for the bless - ings that we share, now to

thee our voic - es raise, in a hymn of grate-ful praise. A - men.

Be Present Here

Mary Youngman Wilson

Dundee
Psalter

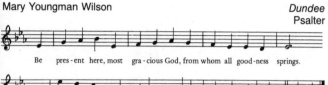

Be pres-ent here, most gra-cious God, from whom all good-ness springs.

Make clean our hearts, and feed our souls on good and joy-ful things. A-men.

Alleluia, Thank You, O Lord

S.M. and B.M.

Sheryl Monroe and Becky Mortvedt

Al - le - lu - ia thank you, O Lord. Al - le - lu - ia thank you, O Lord.

Al - le - lu - ia thank you, O Lord,   for this food we eat.
for this time to share.
for your gra - cious love.
as we cel - e - brate.

Praise and Thanksgiving

Author Unknown

Composer Unknown

This may be sung as a three-part round using entrances indicated.

Praise and thanks-giv - ing let ev - 'ry-one bring, un-to our Fa -ther for

ev - 'ry good thing. All to - geth - er joy - ful - ly sing.

Thank the Lord and Sing His Praise

Author Unknown

Composer Unknown

Thank the Lord and sing his praise; tell ev - 'ry-one what he has done.

Let all who seek the Lord re - joice and proud-ly bear his name.

He re-calls his prom - is - es and leads his peo -ple forth in joy with

shouts of thanks-giv -ing. Al - le - lu - ia. Al - le - lu - ia.

For Health and Strength

Author Unknown

Composer Unknown

English: For health and strength and dai - ly bread, we praise thy name, O Lord.
French: Pour ce re - pas pour tou - te joie, nous tu lu - ons, Sei - gn-eur.
Spanish: Nos da - mos gra - cias, O Señ - or por nues - tra pan de - hoy.

This may be sung as a two-part round using entrances indicated.

Thank Him

S.M. and B.M.

Sheryl Monroe and Becky Mortvedt

1. Let's all join hands and _ thank him. He _ is the
2. Let's all join hands and _ praise him. He _ is the

Lord _ of Hosts. _____ Let's all join hands and _
Lord _ of Hosts. _____ Let's all join hands and _

thank him. He is the Lord of all! _____
praise him. He is the Lord of all! _____

God Is Great, God Is Good

The Hampton Grace, alt.

Marie Pooler

God is great, God is good, and we thank him for this food.

This may be sung as a two-part round using entrances indicated.

Our Table Now with Food Is Spread

L.M.   Lowell Mason

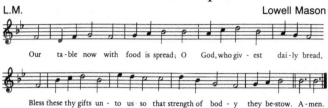

Our ta-ble now with food is spread; O God, who giv-est dai-ly bread,

Bless these thy gifts un-to us so that strength of bod-y they be-stow. A-men.

Great God, We Praise Thy Gracious Care

Author Unknown   *Old Hundredth*
                                                   Louis Bourgeois

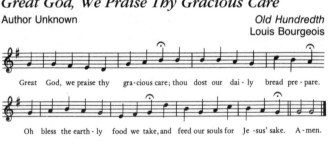

Great God, we praise thy gra-cious care; thou dost our dai-ly bread pre-pare.

Oh bless the earth-ly food we take, and feed our souls for Je-sus' sake. A-men.

For Thy Gifts So Many

Louise M. Oglevee   William G. Oglevee

For thy gifts so— man-y this Thanks-giv-ing— Day,— hear us, lov-ing

Fa-ther, as we glad-ly say,— we— thank thee, we thank thee.

For All Thy Gifts

Author Unknown

Composer Unknown

Morn - ing, ev - 'ning, noon and night, for all thy gifts we thank thee, Lord.

Father of Ours in Heaven Above

Author Unknown

Ignaz Joseph Pleyel

Fa - ther of ours in heav'n a - bove, we praise and thank you

for your love. Our food, our homes, and all we wear

tell of your dai - ly, lov - ing care. A - men.

Oh, Give Thanks

Author Unknown

Composer Unknown

Oh, give thanks, Oh, give thanks, Oh, give thanks un -

to the Lord, for he is gra - cious and his mer -

cy en - dur - eth, en - dur - eth for ev - er.

This may be sung as a two-part round using entrances indicated.

The Board Is Spread

Author Unknown

Composer Unknown

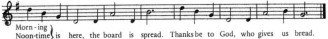

Morn - ing
Noon-time } is here, the board is spread. Thanks be to God, who gives us bread.
Eve - ning

Tak for Maden (Danish, "Thanks for the Meal")

Traditional

Composer Unknown

Tak for ma - den, tak - for ma - den, bless this food we pray.
Tak for ma - den, tak - for ma - den, thank thee, Lord, to - day.

Strength-en, love and guide us, stay thou close be - side us.

Tak for ma - den, tak - for ma - den, thank thee, Lord, to - day. A - men.

We Thank Thee, Dear Father

Mary Youngman Wilson

Away in a Manger
Composer Unknown

We thank thee, dear Fa - ther, for thy gifts of love, for Je - sus, our Sa-vior, our

joy from a - bove. Stay with us and keep us and teach us to share thy

boun - ti - ful good-ness with all ev - 'ry - where. A - men.